GIRL POWER

summersdale

GIRL POWER

Summersdale Publishers Ltd
46 West Street
Chichester
West Sussex
PO19 1RP
UK

www.summersdale.com

Printed and bound in the Czech Republic

ISBN: 978-1-78685-351-6

Substantial discounts on bulk quantities of Summersdale books are available to corporations, professional associations and other organisations. For details contact general enquiries: telephone: +44 (0) 1243 771107, fax: +44 (0) 1243 786300 or email: enquiries@summersdale.com.

TO...

FROM..

ALL WOMEN
ARE NATURALLY

BADASS.

ALICIA KEYS

I have chosen to no longer be apologetic for my femaleness and my femininity.

Chimamanda Ngozi Adichie

YOUNG GIRLS
ARE TOLD... THAT THEY
HAVE TO BE THIS KIND OF
PRINCESS... IF I WAS GOING
TO BE A PRINCESS, I'D BE
A WARRIOR PRINCESS.

Emma Watson

I say if I'm beautiful. I say if I'm strong. You will not determine my story – I will.

Amy Schumer

BETTER TO LIVE ONE YEAR AS A TIGER, THAN A HUNDRED AS A SHEEP.

Madonna

I'M NOT BOSSY, I'M THE BOSS.

Beyoncé

IF ONE GIRL WITH COURAGE
IS A REVOLUTION, IMAGINE
WHAT FEATS WE CAN ACHIEVE
TOGETHER.

Queen Rania of Jordan

There is no
limit to what we,
as women, can
accomplish.

Michelle Obama

I'M A FEMINIST. I'VE BEEN A FEMALE FOR A LONG TIME NOW. IT'D BE STUPID NOT TO BE ON <u>MY OWN SIDE.</u>

MAYA ANGELOU

ACCEPT

WHO YOU ARE.

UNLESS YOU'RE A SERIAL KILLER.

ELLEN DeGENERES

LIVING OUT LOUD IS LIVING
A LIFE THAT'S BIGGER THAN
YOURSELF… YOU LEAVE
SOMETHING ON THIS EARTH
THAT'S **BIGGER THAN YOURSELF.**

Viola Davis

I want [girls] to feel that they can be sassy and full and weird and geeky and smart and independent.

Amy Poehler

IF YOU RETAIN
NOTHING ELSE,
ALWAYS REMEMBER THE
MOST IMPORTANT RULE
OF BEAUTY, WHICH IS:
WHO CARES?

Tina Fey

LET US PICK UP OUR BOOKS AND OUR PENS. THEY ARE THE MOST POWERFUL WEAPONS.

Malala Yousafzai

IF YOU START CARING WHAT PEOPLE THINK, YOU'RE SCREWED.

Natalie Dormer

ONCE YOU FIGURE
OUT WHO YOU ARE AND
WHAT YOU LOVE ABOUT
YOURSELF, IT ALL KIND OF
FALLS INTO PLACE.

Jennifer Aniston

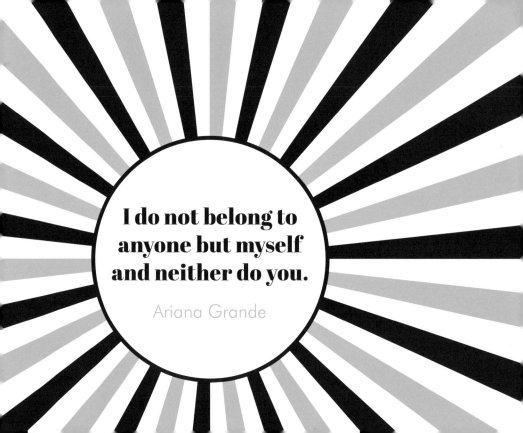

I do not belong to anyone but myself and neither do you.

Ariana Grande

WE ARE EACH MADE DIFFERENTLY, SO FIND WHATEVER FLAW OR IMPERFECTION YOU HAVE AND START EMBRACING IT BECAUSE IT'S <u>PART OF YOU.</u>

DEMI LOVATO

The most beautiful woman in the world is the one who protects and supports other women.

Sandra Bullock

I am a full woman and I'm strong and I'm powerful and I'm beautiful at the same time.

Serena Williams

WHO YOU ARE AUTHENTICALLY
IS ALRIGHT. WHO YOU ARE IS
BEAUTIFUL AND AMAZING.

Laverne Cox

THROUGH THE QUIETEST WHISPERS AND THE LOUDEST MEGAPHONES, [SOCIETY SHOULD] TELL GIRLS THAT THEY ARE UNSTOPPABLE.

MAISIE WILLIAMS

WHO KNOWS WHAT
WOMEN CAN BE WHEN THEY
ARE FINALLY FREE TO BE
THEMSELVES.

Betty Friedan

Real change will come
when powerful women are
less of an exception.

Sheryl Sandberg

GIVE ME A PLACE TO STAND AND I CAN MOVE THE WORLD.

Arianna Huffington

I'll have no man telling me to shave my legs. Shave yours.

Adele

The moment we choose
to love we begin to move
against domination,
against oppression.

bell hooks

[FEMINISM IS]
NOT ABOUT WOMEN
ACTING LIKE MEN. IT'S
ABOUT WOMEN ACTING
LIKE WOMEN AND
BEING SUCCESSFUL.

Zooey Deschanel

I have yet to
hear a man ask
for advice on how
to combine marriage
and a career.

Gloria Steinem

THINK LIKE A QUEEN. A QUEEN IS NOT AFRAID TO FAIL. FAILURE IS ANOTHER STEPPING STONE <u>TO GREATNESS.</u>

OPRAH WINFREY

PART OF BEING
A FEMINIST IS GIVING
OTHER WOMEN THE
FREEDOM TO MAKE
CHOICES YOU MIGHT
NOT NECESSARILY
MAKE YOURSELF.

Lena Dunham

A man told me that for a woman, I was very opinionated. I said, 'For a man, you're kind of ignorant.'

Anne Hathaway

WOMEN AND GIRLS SHOULD BE ABLE TO DETERMINE THEIR OWN FUTURE, NO MATTER WHERE THEY'RE BORN.

Melinda Gates

I SEE MY BODY AS AN INSTRUMENT, RATHER THAN AN ORNAMENT.

Alanis Morissette

OF COURSE I AM NOT WORRIED ABOUT INTIMIDATING MEN. THE TYPE OF MAN WHO WILL BE INTIMIDATED BY ME IS EXACTLY THE TYPE OF MAN I HAVE <u>NO INTEREST IN.</u>

CHIMAMANDA NGOZI ADICHIE

You are allowed to be radical and have strong thoughts that others might not agree with.

Alicia Keys

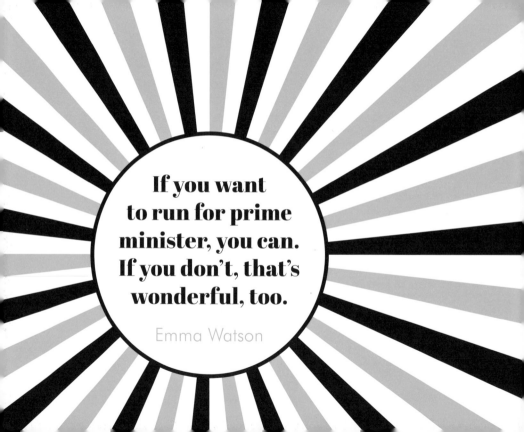

If you want
to run for prime
minister, you can.
If you don't, that's
wonderful, too.

Emma Watson

THE SUCCESS OF EVERY
WOMAN SHOULD BE THE
INSPIRATION TO ANOTHER. WE
SHOULD **RAISE EACH OTHER UP.**

Serena Williams

I am not who I sleep with.
I am not my weight. I am not
my mother. I am myself.

Amy Schumer

I'd rather be strong and happy than be what society thinks is thin and perfect and be miserable.

Demi Lovato

THE THING EVERYONE
SHOULD REALISE IS
THAT THE KEY TO
HAPPINESS IS BEING
HAPPY BY YOURSELF
AND <u>FOR YOURSELF.</u>

ELLEN DeGENERES

THERE'S NO
RACE, NO RELIGION,
NO CLASS SYSTEM, NO
COLOUR – NOTHING – NO
SEXUAL ORIENTATION, THAT
MAKES US BETTER THAN
ANYONE ELSE. WE'RE ALL
DESERVING OF LOVE.

Sandra Bullock

I'm gonna look back on my life and say that I enjoyed it – and I lived it for me.

Rihanna

YOU CAN'T BE HESITANT ABOUT WHO YOU ARE.

Viola Davis

Please never stop believing that fighting for what's right is worth it.

Hillary Clinton

No country can ever truly flourish if it stifles the potential of its women.

Michelle Obama

DIFFERENT IS
GOOD. WHEN SOMEONE
TELLS YOU THAT YOU ARE
DIFFERENT, SMILE AND
HOLD YOUR HEAD UP
AND BE PROUD.

Angelina Jolie

I THINK YOU CAN BE DEFIANT AND REBELLIOUS AND STILL BE STRONG AND **POSITIVE**.

MADONNA

No matter where you're from, your dreams are valid.

Lupita Nyong'o

We cannot all succeed when half of us are held back.

Malala Yousafzai

By doing the work to love
ourselves more, I believe we
will love each other better.

Laverne Cox

I'M OVER TRYING TO FIND THE 'ADORABLE' WAY TO STATE

MY OPINION.

JENNIFER LAWRENCE

THE MOST COMMON
WAY PEOPLE GIVE UP THEIR
POWER IS BY THINKING THEY
DON'T HAVE ANY.

Alice Walker

A truly equal world would be one where women ran half our countries and companies and men ran half our homes.

Sheryl Sandberg

MY DREAM WAS
TO BE THE BEST TENNIS
PLAYER IN THE WORLD.
NOT THE BEST 'FEMALE'
TENNIS PLAYER IN
THE WORLD.

Serena Williams

THE RULES ARE WHATEVER YOU WANT THEM TO BE.

Tina Fey

WE ARE STRONGER WHEN WE LISTEN, AND SMARTER WHEN WE SHARE.

Queen Rania of Jordan

WHEN A WOMAN
RISES UP IN GLORY, HER
ENERGY IS MAGNETIC AND
HER SENSE OF POSSIBILITY
CONTAGIOUS.

Marianne Williamson

WHEN A MAN GIVES HIS OPINION, HE'S A MAN. WHEN A WOMAN GIVES HER OPINION, SHE'S A B***H.

BETTE DAVIS

I don't have time to worry about something as petty as what I look like.

Adele

I THINK THE BEST ROLE MODELS FOR WOMEN ARE PEOPLE WHO ARE FRUITFULLY AND CONFIDENTLY <u>THEMSELVES.</u>

MERYL STREEP

I just love
bossy women...
To me, bossy... means
somebody's passionate
and engaged and
ambitious and doesn't
mind leading.

Amy Poehler

PEOPLE GIVE ME SUCH A HARD
TIME BECAUSE I DON'T WEAR
DRESSES. WHAT'S THAT GOT TO
DO WITH **ANYTHING?**

Ellen DeGeneres

No one can make you feel inferior without your consent.

Eleanor Roosevelt

IT'S GOING TO
BE OKAY. NO MATTER
HOW HARD YOUR ROCK
BOTTOM IS, YOU CAN RISE
ABOVE IT AND YOU CAN
COME BACK.

Demi Lovato

**ALWAYS CHOOSE PEOPLE
THAT CHALLENGE YOU AND
ARE SMARTER THAN YOU.
ALWAYS BE THE STUDENT.**

Sandra Bullock

Girl power is almost more powerful and more special than anything we are competing for.

Selena Gomez

IF YOUR DREAMS DO NOT SCARE YOU, THEY ARE NOT BIG ENOUGH.

Ellen Johnson Sirleaf

I WOULD RATHER
BE A REBEL
THAN A SLAVE.

EMMELINE PANKHURST

The thing women have yet to learn is nobody gives you power. You just take it.

Roseanne Barr

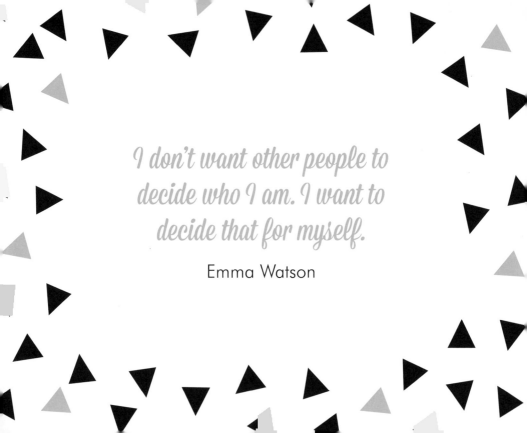

I don't want other people to decide who I am. I want to decide that for myself.

Emma Watson

THE MOST
POWERFUL THING IS
FOR WOMEN NOT JUST
TO BE THE BENEFICIARIES
OF THE CHANGE, BUT
TO BE AGENTS OF IT.

Blake Lively

BEING YOURSELF
AND BEING TRUE TO
WHAT MAKES YOU
HAPPY IS THE MOST
IMPORTANT THING.

ZOOEY DESCHANEL

[Every woman should be] absolute mistress of her own body.

Margaret Sanger

I NEVER UNDERESTIMATED
MYSELF. AND I NEVER SAW
ANYTHING WRONG WITH
AMBITION.

Angela Merkel

MY MOTTO IS: I'M ALIVE, SO THAT MEANS I CAN DO ANYTHING.

VENUS WILLIAMS

PERFECT IS VERY BORING,
AND IF YOU HAPPEN TO HAVE
A DIFFERENT LOOK, THAT'S
A CELEBRATION OF HUMAN
NATURE... IF WE WERE ALL
SYMMETRICAL AND PERFECT,
LIFE WOULD BE VERY DULL.

Natalie Dormer

If a woman never lets herself go, how will she ever know how far she might have got?

Germaine Greer

DO YOUR THING AND DON'T CARE IF THEY LIKE IT.

Tina Fey

People ask why I am confident.
It's because my parents raised
me with the entitlement of a
tall, blonde, white man.

Mindy Kaling

EDUCATE A WOMAN
AND YOU EDUCATE HER
FAMILY. EDUCATE A
GIRL AND YOU CHANGE
THE FUTURE.

QUEEN RANIA OF JORDAN

I DON'T HAVE
ANY TIME TO STAY UP ALL
NIGHT WORRYING ABOUT
WHAT SOMEONE WHO
DOESN'T LOVE ME HAS
TO SAY ABOUT ME.

Viola Davis

The question
isn't who is going to
let me; it's who is
going to stop me.

Ayn Rand

Feminism isn't about making women stronger. Women are already strong. It's about changing the way the world perceives that strength.

G. D. Anderson

**The formula of happiness
and success is just, being
actually yourself, in the most
vivid possible way you can.**

Meryl Streep

I AM NOT FREE
WHILE ANY WOMAN IS
UNFREE, EVEN WHEN
HER SHACKLES ARE
VERY DIFFERENT
FROM <u>MY OWN.</u>

AUDRE LORDE

FAILURE ISN'T AN OPTION. I'VE
ERASED THE WORD 'FEAR'
FROM MY VOCABULARY, AND
I THINK WHEN YOU ERASE FEAR,
YOU CAN'T FAIL.

Alicia Keys

THERE'S POWER IN LOOKING SILLY AND NOT CARING THAT YOU DO.

Amy Poehler

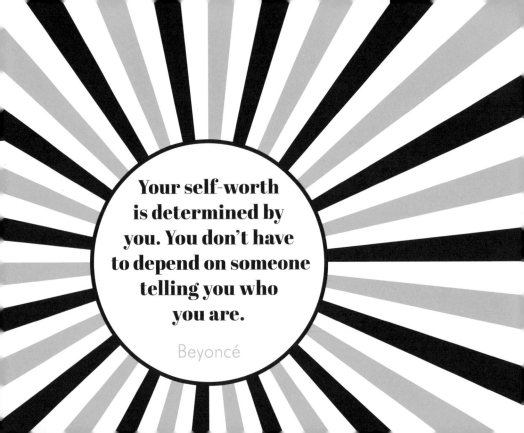

BEAUTY IS NOT BETWEEN A SIZE 0 AND A SIZE 8. IT'S NOT A NUMBER AT ALL.

Ellen DeGeneres

I MYSELF HAVE NEVER BEEN
ABLE TO FIND OUT PRECISELY
WHAT FEMINISM IS: I ONLY
KNOW THAT PEOPLE CALL ME A
FEMINIST WHENEVER I EXPRESS
SENTIMENTS THAT DIFFERENTIATE
ME FROM **A DOORMAT.**

Rebecca West

TALL, THIN, CURVY, SHORT, WHATEVER YOU ARE, YOU ARE

BEAUTIFUL.

DEMI LOVATO

I WANT TO BE
RESPECTED IN ALL OF
MY FEMALENESS BECAUSE
I DESERVE TO BE.

Chimamanda
Ngozi Adichie

IF YOUR HUSBAND IS CHEATING ON YOU, IT DOESN'T MEAN THAT YOU NEED TO GET PRETTIER – IT MEANS <u>HE'S A SCUMBAG.</u>

JESSICA VALENTI

YOU ARE
NOT DEFINED BY
AN INSTAGRAM
PHOTO, BY A LIKE, BY A
COMMENT. THAT DOES
NOT DEFINE YOU.

Selena Gomez

I just don't believe in perfection. But I do believe in saying, 'This is who I am and look at me not being perfect!'

Kate Winslet

MY FEARS CAME TRUE: PEOPLE CALLED ME FAT AND HIDEOUS, AND I LIVED.

Lena Dunham

My great hope for us as young women is to start being kinder to ourselves.

Emma Stone

IN THE FUTURE, THERE WILL BE
NO FEMALE LEADERS. THERE
WILL **JUST BE LEADERS.**

Sheryl Sandberg

We've begun
to raise daughters
more like sons... but
few have the courage to
raise our sons more like
our daughters.

Gloria Steinem

You can be whatever size you are, and you can be beautiful both inside and out.

Serena Williams

The men liked to put me down as the best woman painter. I think I'm one of the best painters.

Georgia O'Keeffe

DON'T LIVE
SOMEONE ELSE'S LIFE
AND SOMEONE ELSE'S IDEA
OF WHAT WOMANHOOD
IS. WOMANHOOD IS
EVERYTHING THAT'S
INSIDE OF YOU.

Viola Davis

WE NEED TO LAUGH AT THE HATERS AND SYMPATHISE WITH THEM. THEY CAN SCREAM AS LOUD AS THEY WANT. WE CAN'T HEAR THEM BECAUSE WE ARE <u>GETTING S**T DONE.</u>

AMY SCHUMER

You must never
be fearful about
what you are doing
when it is right.

Rosa Parks

Women speaking up for themselves and for those around them is the strongest force we have to change the world.

Melinda Gates

Men are not the enemy, but the fellow victims. The real enemy is women's denigration of themselves.

Betty Friedan

I'M NOT THE NEXT USAIN BOLT OR MICHAEL PHELPS. I'M THE FIRST SIMONE BILES.

Simone Biles

IF A MAN WHISTLES AT YOU, DO NOT RESPOND. YOU ARE A LADY, NOT A DOG.

Adele

As long as women are using class or race power to dominate other women, feminist sisterhood cannot be fully realised.

bell hooks

WE ARE STILL
WORKING AT TRYING TO
OVERCOME THE FEAR THAT
POWER AND WOMANLINESS
ARE **MUTUALLY EXCLUSIVE.**

Arianna Huffington

When you undervalue what you do, the world will undervalue who you are.

Oprah Winfrey

I JUST WANT WOMEN TO ALWAYS FEEL IN CONTROL. BECAUSE WE'RE CAPABLE – WE'RE <u>SO CAPABLE.</u>

NICKI MINAJ

I AM TIRED OF LIVING IN A WORLD WHERE WOMEN ARE MOSTLY REFERRED TO BY A MAN'S PAST, PRESENT OR **FUTURE POSSESSION.**

Ariana Grande

We should stop calling
feminists 'feminists'
and just start calling people
who aren't feminist 'sexist'.

Maisie Williams

HUMAN RIGHTS ARE
WOMEN'S RIGHTS, AND
WOMEN'S RIGHTS ARE
HUMAN RIGHTS.

Hillary Clinton

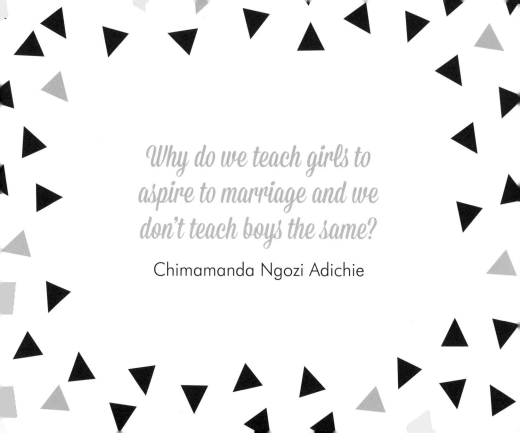

Why do we teach girls to aspire to marriage and we don't teach boys the same?

Chimamanda Ngozi Adichie

I'M TOUGH, I'M AMBITIOUS, AND I KNOW EXACTLY WHAT I WANT. IF THAT MAKES ME A B***H,

OKAY.

MADONNA

WE DO NOT NEED MAGIC TO CHANGE THE WORLD; WE CARRY ALL THE POWER WE NEED INSIDE OURSELVES ALREADY.

J. K. ROWLING

MY BEAUTY IS NOT ABOUT HOW I LOOK. MY BEAUTY IS ABOUT MY HEART AND SOUL.

Laverne Cox

**We all have our imperfections.
But I'm human, and you know, it's
important to concentrate on other
qualities besides outer beauty.**

Beyoncé

I raise up my voice – not so I can shout, but so that those without a voice can be heard.

Malala Yousafzai

BOTH MEN AND WOMEN SHOULD FEEL FREE TO BE SENSITIVE. BOTH MEN AND WOMEN SHOULD FEEL FREE TO BE STRONG.

Emma Watson

TO GIRLS AND WOMEN
EVERYWHERE, I ISSUE A SIMPLE
INVITATION. MY SISTERS, MY
DAUGHTERS, MY FRIENDS:
FIND YOUR VOICE.

Ellen Johnson Sirleaf

If you're interested in finding out more about our books,
find us on Facebook at **Summersdale Publishers**
and follow us on Twitter at **@Summersdale**.

www.summersdale.com